Facts About the Wolverine

By Lisa Strattin

© 2019 Lisa Strattin

merry Christmas,
Chris! & Panda
Dec. 2020

Facts for Kids Picture Books by Lisa Strattin

Little Blue Penguin, Vol 92

Chipmunk, Vol 5

Frilled Lizard, Vol 39

Blue and Gold Macaw, Vol 13

Poison Dart Frogs, Vol 50

Blue Tarantula, Vol 115

African Elephants, Vol 8

Amur Leopard, Vol 89

Sabre Tooth Tiger, Vol 167

Baboon, Vol 174

Sign Up for New Release Emails Here

http://LisaStrattin.com/subscribe-here

Monthly Surprise Box

http://KidCraftsByLisa.com

** COVER PHOTO **

** ADDITIONAL PHOTOS **

3

Contents

INTRODUCTION

The wolverine is a medium sized mammal that, even though it looks like a bear, is most closely related to the weasel. They are known to be strong and vicious and have immense strength in comparison to its size.

CHARACTERISTICS

Wolverines are territorial animals and they fight other wolverines to defend their territory from intruders. They are not particularly fast movers, though they have been observed running at a speed of 30 miles per hour when necessary. They do not chase or stalk their prey, they usually wait and ambush prey that gets close enough to them to catch.

They are good climbers and often rest in trees, and then pounce on their prey from the trees or large rocks.

APPEARANCE

The wolverine has very sharp teeth and powerful jaws that it uses to crush large bones. They also are able to eat meat that has been frozen in the Arctic winter. The wolverine also has five long, powerful claws on each foot that it uses to catch prey and to defend itself from predators and other wolverines. They also use these claws for climbing and digging.

Like the skunk, the wolverine has a strong-smelling fluid called musk used to warn others to stay away. They also have a thick coat of brown fur that protects them from the freezing cold temperatures where they live. With their large feet, it is able to move across the soft snow.

LIFE STAGES

The female wolverine has one litter every two or three years. She digs her own den with tunnels in a snowdrift that is usually near piles of rocks. After a gestation period of nearly 2 months, she gives birth to a small litter of baby wolverines, generally 2 or 3, that are called kits. The mother nurses her kits until they are around 10 weeks old. The young are then big enough and strong enough to start learning to hunt for themselves.

LIFE SPAN

Wolverines usually live to between 8 and 13 years old, although some wolverine individuals in captivity have been known to nearly reach the age of 20!

SIZE

Most adult wolverines are between 2 to 3 feet long and weigh 22 to 40 pounds.

HABITAT

The wolverine is found throughout Canada, Europe, parts of North America and the Arctic Circle. In these areas, the wolverines inhabit mountainous regions and dense forests. They have been known to roam into more open areas like plains and farms when they are looking for food.

Wolverines prefer colder areas for their homes because they use the snow for dens as well as a safe place to store their food.

DIET

The wolverine generally eats mice, rats and other small mammals, as well as birds and eggs during the summer months, when these are in abundance. During the winter however, when snow covers the ground, the wolverine hunts larger animals such as reindeer, sheep and moose.

Even though they are able to hunt down and kill animals that are much bigger than themselves, the wolverines prefer to scavenge the kills of other animals such as wolves and bears. The wolverine allows the larger predators to hunt the prey down and it then chases the hunter away by showing its teeth and growling fiercely. Once the hunter runs away, the wolverine is left to eat the kill.

ENEMIES

The mountain lion, wolf, and bear are predators of the wolverine. However, people building roads and encroaching on their natural habitats (forestry and oil and gas exploration) are the biggest threat to the wolverines survival.

SUITABILITY AS PETS

The wolverine is a vicious and a meat-eating predator. It is not considered to be a good choice as a pet. They are also aggressive and territorial. If you want to see wolverines, it would be better for you to visit your local zoo and watch them there.

COLOR ME

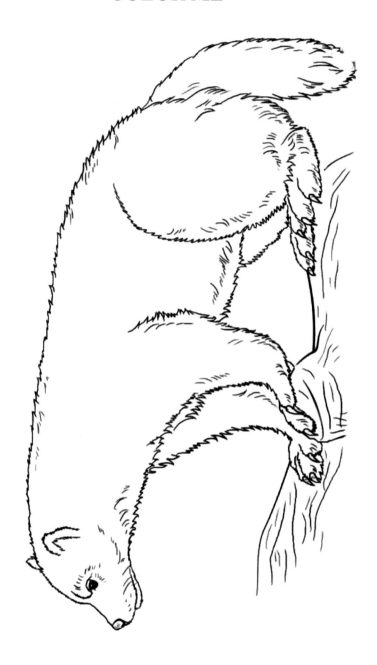

COLOR ME

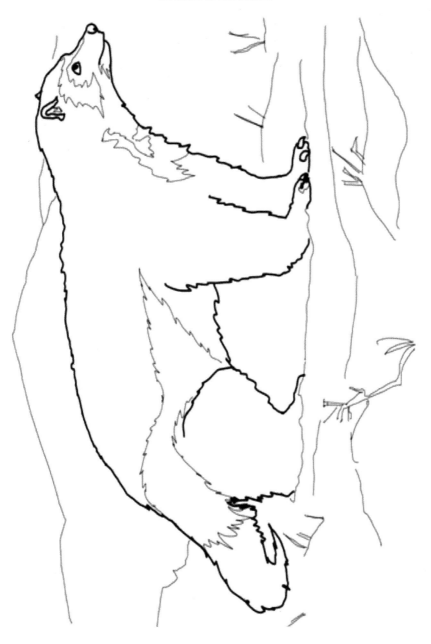

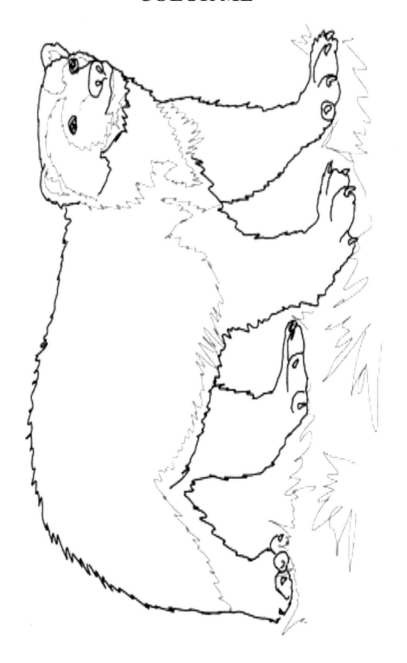

COLOR ME

Please leave me a review here:

http://lisastrattin.com/Review-Vol-236

For more Kindle Downloads Visit Lisa Strattin Author Page on Amazon Author Central

http://amazon.com/author/lisastrattin

To see upcoming titles, visit my website at LisaStrattin.com– all books available on kindle!

http://lisastrattin.com

PLUSH WOLVERINE TOY

You can get one by copying and pasting this link into your browser:

http://lisastrattin.com/PlushWolverine

MONTHLY SURPRISE BOX

Get yours by copying and pasting this link into your browser

http://KidCraftsByLisa.com

Made in the USA
Monee, IL
21 December 2020